The Sunshine Diaries

By Margorie Clemente

I
Ghost Child

the beginning

I am a toddler. I sit in my high chair and watch the sun pour in through the wall-length windows. The yellow light stretches across the kitchen floor like a yawn and nestles on my toes.

Villy, the babysitter, swivels her hips and shimmies near the counter, doing a quick little merengue shuffle with her feet. Today she finally decides to shower, picks up her oily hair, puts on her mommy face, cooks, and dances.

She waltzes over and glowers down at me. My toes curl; they grow cold, bereft of the sun's warmth. Her shadow spills over me and my spine turns to ice. With one swift motion, her hand cups my face, and she hisses.

Stop staring at me and eat. Swallow.

My eyes cut to her soft face, the peach fuzz on her cheeks scintillating in the sun.

Then she gazes at her blonde children shrieking just beyond the sliding glass door. They thrash and laugh under the sun's gentle scorch in their kiddie pool. The sun bursts through the ocean blue plastic.

Villy's eyes are tight and glaring. I fold into myself like a napkin, shrink into my high chair and shiver violently. My thighs squeeze together as I suck in my gut, holding in a river of urine.

My eyes flit across the room desperately, searching for something to alleviate the white-hot burn of her wild, gray eyes—the green-tinted pickle jar enflamed by the sun, the gallon of milk rotting beneath it—anything.

You want to be outside, don't you?

She sneers through flaring nostrils. *You wish could play in that pool with my babies.*

A film of sweat covers my tiny palms, so I press them flat over my thighs—eyes dropped. She nudges my head away sharply with her knuckles against my chin and breathes out into my face.

Keep your neck turned that way; you're not allowed to look at my babies or me. Now, eat. She smells like the orange rice and corned beef that sizzles on the stove.

Outside, her children sing.

Here, I sit in my own filth, soaking in my huggies.

And yet, the sun still gleams.

pastel colors

she remembers that house in shades of blue and
gray
a childhood memory of staring at pastel-colored
walls forever

she is terrified of pasty, baby colors

those colors mean something:
warm milk, a patchy, stuffed lamb, a barney
cassette tape,
an old rocking horse with chipped paint—

the one that
sat in front of the TV—the one she was
only sometimes
allowed to ride

she has nightmares about a big-boned,
bold woman with a long, gentle jaw

nightmares of chewing on a blanket
to alleviate the hunger pangs

of soaking in a cold, piss-filled tub
and tiny, pruny fingers

child's play

I choked on a Chinese ball as a child
and I remember the way it felt, lodged in my throat

and the way my mother let out this unnerving
howl—
grabbed a fistful of my hair and dragged me across
the
apartment floor like an animal

her fists came down hard on the bedroom door
to wake my father from his drunken, afternoon
slumber

while my mother tightened her fists, hauling me up
and began to pump hard in the center of my ribs

someone calmly tilted my head back and pried my
jaw open
and as I gagged and thrashed
I was starting to see spots...

my father curled his index finger and carefully
dipped it
to the back of my throat

suddenly, the toy seemed to fly out like projectile
vomit
along with a spittle of blood that I'd coughed up

onto the wooden floors

my father saved my life
I still don't know how to feel about that—
about *any of it,* really

I just remember how it felt to realize that I was
going to die

The Superhero Who Gave Up

Some time in the year '96

My father

was what Superman

would have been,

if he were possessed

by Bacardi and Jim Beam

on the weekends.

The man swept me

off my feet—

no date,

cape,

and no catch phrase.

Admittedly,

my father was a beautiful man.

Still is.

He's not a six-foot tall guy,

but he's got a grin

that made my teachers and babysitters

swoon (and a little something more).

Chestnut lips

curled over

an uneasy,

perfect grin

and a pair of warm,

almond-shaped eyes.

Even on his worst days,

the guy is Denzel Washington.

Always immaculately dressed,

hair and beard trimmed to perfection.

Smooth-talking punk—

can catch you so quick.

Before you know it,

you've found yourself

knee-deep

in a pile

of horse shit.

Some illegal, get-rich-quick pyramid.

And so his shaking,

rough,

brown hands

were tucked under my pits.

He whirled me

around the room

like a rag doll.

Doing this

dangerous,

dizzying

dance

in the middle of our living room.

The bastard

tripped over

my Polly Pockets, cassettes, blankets, stuffed animals

and knocked over

my sippy cup.

The only light now

was the Technicolor glow

from the TV below us.

It made me feel

sick.

My mother

fluttered about the room

like a nervous

      little butterfly.

She pleaded

in a low

and trembling voice.

Holding her arms out in front of her

as though ready to catch

one of her glass unicorns

from falling

off the edge

                of

                        the

                                table.

You put her down, Rudy.

You put her down now! Or so help me God—

He breathed

into my face—

my eyes

stinging

as my fingernails

buried into his black

leather jacket—clinging onto him

for dear life.

Who do you love more?

He drawled, demanded.

His tongue thick and heavy

with Bacardi—

eyes glistening.

Me or mommy?

Summer of 2000

My father

clambered out of his friend's

trailer

and swung around a Corona

in his fist.

His friend's wife's name

was Margarita,

and apparently

she made killer Margaritas.

She had a clumsy walk,

bony knees,

and was followed

by a constant

cloud

of smoke.

She half jokingly

offered me a Margarita.

I must have been about seven.

She beckoned me

over,

puffing on a

Virginia Slim

balanced between her long fingers.

Margarita pulled

at her purple pleather skirt

and licked her pursed pink lips

at my father.

I didn't like Margarita

because I could see

her nipples

through her tank top.

And she was always

running her desiccated hands

through her frazzled,

bleach blonde head

and looking around at her sides

all the time.

I didn't think I would actually

like Margaritas either.

My mother

always pulled me close

to her breast

whenever Margarita was near.

My father watched me carefully,

tossed his head back,

and guffawed.

That night,

in their trailer-park neighborhood,

I had my first boyfriend.

It would be a miracle

if I remembered the kid's name,

but I always think *John*

for some reason.

He drove me

around the blonde fields

in a pink Barbie sports car.

All of his friends wore overalls.

He had a dog

who wore a scary semblance

to Wishbone.

I can make him talk.

You wanna see?

We kissed

under the jungle gym.

It was sloppy—

tasted like grass

and fruit loops.

I raced back to the trailer.

Before turning away,

Margarita winked

one

wrinkled

eye at me

and planted a wet kiss

on my temple.

I couldn't wait

to get into the car

and wipe off her saliva

and my lipstick-stained

face with my sleeve.

On the way home,

my mother seemed to grumble

at my father

the entire time.

As I gazed

out of the window

and the sky erupted

into smoke and fiery rainbows

I suddenly remembered—

I think it was the Fourth of July.

Some other time in 2000

In the wake of my nightmare,

he towered over my bed.

His shaky, brown hands all warm.

And like some twisted, sleepy Superman,

he whisked me off

into the darkness of the kitchen

placing me up onto the counter.

Half of the floor bathed in the moonlight,

and the churn in my stomach

vanished as the hum

of the microwave lulled me.

As did the sugary, creamy texture that touched my lips

—milk from a Minnie Mouse mug.

I folded into his chest.

The stubble on his chin

felt like grains of sand

through my fingers.

And grazed against my shoulder

in an itchy, familiar way.

I was comfortable in his grip

just this way.

Christmas Eve, 2004

My father crawled

up the stairs from our

basement

ready to topple over.

I stared up at him

once he'd straightened himself upright again—

tempted to kick his teeth

in.

He demanded

that I shut up

and get the karaoke machine.

I wanna sing! We should sing!

So I shut up,

and got the karaoke machine.

I spent hour

after hour

after

hour

going up and down the steps

getting him his beer.

Another beer. Another shot. One more.

He jabbed his knuckles fiercely

into his chest and then

he bellowed,

I am the monster of all aliens!

Finally, he crawled

into the upstairs bathroom,

locked himself in,

and slumped into the tub—his heels slipping and sliding.

My mother's fists

came down hard

at the bathroom door.

You'll drown in there, and I'll let you!

Rudy, open up!

Sometime in the later 2000s

Everyday my parents' moods were like rolling dice—

Some days

they would sit outside

on our poorly designed patio,

if the weather was nice,

and paint birdhouses together.

Everyone thought they were so *cute*.

And our neighbors

would watch them,

then turn to their partners lovingly and say:

I would love to grow older with you that way

with stars

in their eyes.

Some nights

when the weather wasn't as agreeable,

Mom's arthritic fingers

would fumble with fat crocheting needles,

tears dribbling from her face—

soaking the yarn

of a scarf

she was making

for me.

Meanwhile,

my old man

would shrink into the basement—

He would drink

until he didn't care

who the hell we were

anymore.

And I hated him

for trying to pick us off,

Mom and me,

like old scabs.

And everyday,

at least to me,

even my parents' relationship

made fairy tales

seem believable.

In the mornings,

Mom said

the stench of alcohol

would seep from his pores

until the bedroom was unbearable.

Among the many insults

he showered us with,

one particular morning he spat,

I'm tired of living a mediocre life,

and then gave a long, wistful sigh.

Like he was the one who was suffering

in this relationship

—if it was one at all.

"Fighting vainly the old ennui,"

the way old blue eyes would have sung it.

And I just couldn't believe him.

I have been scared to death

ever since

to love another man just enough

in fear that he will look at me one day

in that same way

and slice me open

just to bury his insecurities inside of me

and suddenly decide that *I* am the one

who is too mediocre for *him*.

Because I was the only witness—

the only one who saw

the way

that it

      defeated

my mother

when he said that

to her.

I

was the only one

who saw how my father

slowly

sucked the light

out of her eyes

with his words.

Fourth of July, 2010

There was only one girl at this party

who was my age.

And she was holding

one of those

electronically programmed

babies.

It was for her summer class.

Sucks to suck,

I thought.

She left early,

so we didn't get to really

bond.

My mother wore

a tight smile, refusing

an alcoholic drink.

She sat with the wives

of *machistas*.

Wives who linked arms,

drank too much and talked shit together.

Who hated their husbands

but hated each other even more—

which was why

they all smiled anyway

and took selfies together,

but constantly sized each other up like pissed off cats.

At their table,

it was like watching

a high school clique.

For the first time,

my mother joined the women

in a chorus of laughter at jokes

she didn't quite catch

or even really care about—

all for my dad.

My father's best friend, Palo,

stumbled over his feet

around the pool table

in the center of the basement.

My head swam around

beer bellies,

cologne,

Cuban cigars,

and open-toed sandals.

Palo pulled me in

by my waist

and twirled with me.

Our foreheads almost touched.

His face was oily,

so I leaned back.

He had a small,

gold hoop earring

in his left ear.

His breath was warm

on my face,

my breasts pressed against his chest.

His shirt was damp

with sweat and I could feel

his boner probing my thigh.

These people's housedog looks like a fuckin' sheep!

He pointed at the water Portuguese dog with the
cropped tail.

Palo bellowed, laughed hysterically—

garbling his words.

He shoved a pool stick

at me and demanded softly,

Play a little pool with us, mama.

Why are you acting shy?

His hazel eyes flashed over me,

hungry and curious.

I wriggled out of his arms,

shrugging away from him

and nudged the pool stick back at him,

glaring.

My chest tightened,

fighting back tears that

threatened at my lashes.

I sat on a stool

and stared down at the beer

sticking in between my toes.

My father swayed,

balancing himself

on a pool stick

and watched us carefully

beneath his brow

with a cigar

sticking out between his lips.

I thought I saw him smirking.

Sweet Dreams

I was born to wear flip-flops
and feel the thick plastic chafing
the skin between my big toe and
my middle toe—
born to show off my freshly done pedicure
and bat my mascara-caked lashes upward
to flirt with the sun.

And I already talked about how
I was born to never catch a robin,
in all of its velvety, crimson coat and fleeting
glory—
an unobtainable, fiery little angel.
And even though I spent hours
on a summer's afternoon
fixing bird traps with my father
trying to take what wasn't even mine,
I always knew deep down it would never be.

Some days we contemplated
on grabbing our BB rifle and
would wait at the window, watching eagerly.
Then we backed out the very last minute
when we saw that tiny, vermillion creature
bathing itself in the pink evening sunlight,
fluttering its wings nervously as water from the
fountain
sprung from its feathers like slivers of ice.

I was born to kiss boys on balmy summer nights
with a little bravery from Bacardi on my breath
and then regret it in the mornings.

I was born to tell a story
with the tip of a cigarette burning between my
lips—
all glassy-eyed and singing off-key
and wondering where the hell my life is headed.

I was born to drink in the nightlife

with salt and lemon on the side.

I was born to join the party
and make everyone there raise a toast
to whatever it is they're all anxious about
and everyone will cheer—
hoping for something good to beam down
on their lives
no matter the situation they're in.
And all of them will believe in something
with all of that liquor swimming in their system,
dripping from their throbbing pores
and happily filling in their hearts and stomachs—
their livers crying out for help all the while.

My Girl

We first met when the sun was beginning to set in the west. I waited anxiously, looking in all directions. My eyes darted this way and that across a moderately-sized yard. I could hear the cars whizzing down the avenue on the other side of the block. I could hear the ice cream truck. I could hear—footsteps. And that was when I saw her. She was wearing a funny, short-sleeved shirt and long pants. A uniform, maybe? She was this bouncing girl with unruly curls that brushed up against my nose as she hugged me. But she was just a kid, hardly developing. Barely living.

So I was home again. She—they welcomed me with a much needed, familiar, and warm embrace. I was desperate. I longed for a family. I longed for touch. I needed to be needed. And here they were in all their black and white hue-ish glory, a perfect and broken family of three, standing before a pale pink, brick house and twisted curtains.

I knew her for what felt like a lifetime, even though I wasn't there when she was born. Even her mother in stubbornness learned to grow fond of my presence. Sometimes she would nudge me away irritably with the back of her hand as she plucked her own brows on the sofa, holding up a mirror to her face. But moments she later would apologetically place her hand at the back of my neck. And with a smile in her voice she'd say, hey, you.

That beautiful brown girl with the curls—we went for really long walks, and that was my favorite part of the day. Since most days I felt shut up and trapped, I pictured her coming home. Seeing her was my favorite. Smelling her was my favorite. She was my favorite.

I thought of the sound of that doorknob clicking and twisting open. Then there she was, standing before me. Sometimes she was in tears, and other days she was beaming. But all in all, she was always shaking when she saw me. I trembled too. It was a bodily function I simply couldn't control unless she demanded it to cease on command.

I listened to her. Well, I almost always listened to her. Her room was the one I watched the most because I was her most precious vigilante. I'd often poke my head in and ask her—in my own way—if she was all right. She would only grin and toss her thin arms around me. Sometimes she sobbed, and other times she squealed out this strident laughter. I'd cock my head as though to avoid it, but eventually I absorbed the sound and fell in love with it.

That was my biggest mistake; I grew attached.

She taught me many nifty little things to get chores around the house done more efficiently like holding the dirty dishrag as she half-assed rinsed the dishes. Sometimes I even peeked in while she showered. She would shriek with laughter, shaking her towel at me playfully,

Oh, you nasty! Get out!

Now, her father was a different story. Her father's barks were worse than mine whenever he yelled at the girl.

Put that down! Stop that! Sit down! Come here!

Many times I would watch him pack his things in haste and storm out of the house, swearing he would never return. That sweet, brown girl cried as snot streamed down her face. She begged him with tired, aged eyes for him not to leave. He would callously turn his back on us and duck out of the back door like the coward he was.

Meanwhile, I watched from the bedroom doorway as the mother sobbed over a ball of tangled, multi-colored yarn and gigantic sticks that weaved seamlessly between her fingers. She made a lot of those warm, fuzzy balls for the sobbing girl.

I knew that girl more than I knew my own self. When her shoulders closed in and her head hung low, I was at her side. My heart twisted whenever she touched me. I didn't understand if it was a health problem or if I was just really happy.

With the stroke of her skinny fingers through my coarse tufts, the corners of her lips would break out into a grin. An unusual smile that reached her dark eyes—eyes dark like two black suns.

When the air around her was heavy, she ran to me—her curls leaping and shouting at me, her clumsy, bow-legged jog thrust me into a dizzying love.

And still, all day and every day of the week I felt imprisoned—forgotten. Neglect was the least to say of all things done to my petty and miserable existence in that household. I stared through the black, cross-hatched bars before me and wondered if I was left alone here to starve forever—left here to sit beside my own shit and piss and vomit and watered down left overs that made my stomach roll in on itself every time I glanced at it.

I taught myself to listen to the house breathe out. I sat on the velvet sofa, curled up, with my cheek pressed up against the cool glass of our windows. I pet the red velvet beneath the warmth of my thighs like a kitten and felt a grand purr gradually erupt beneath me. The sofa's breath reeked of Cuban cigar smoke and Corona.

The rain was gray, rug was gray, her mother's new flyaway hairs, plucked by old tweezers strewn all over the seat lying across from me like confetti, even looked gray. The wind blew, the house inhaled and let out a groan, and her light tiptoes stretched across the wooden floors like a yawn—but the pelting rain against the glass was still tracing in my brain.

You know, even that dining table draped in that tattered cloth splattered with rich burgundy stains were starting to look like gray blobs to me right about now. And I think there was even a little bit of gray growing on those wretched placemats with crusts of old Thanksgiving orange rice and dried broth stuck to the surface. God, how I loved sneaking mouthfuls of her mother's food when she wasn't looking.

While she cooked, it was the girl who scooped up a metal spoonful of the rice. I wolfed down the contents, pleased.

Those were the same placemats the girl despised and dropped a few tears over when she accidentally shattered one of her mother's glass cups.

I stood over the shards of glass and the hairs at the back of my neck rose on their ends when I heard the furious shouts of her mother.

Get away from there and out of my sight! I don't want to see either of you for the rest of the night!

I bowed my head and followed after the girl sheepishly.

Then there were those dusty, chipped candleholders that once kindled many family dinners of a blue, awkward silence that hung over us like a thick miasma.

Early one morning, I remember lounging about near the sofa and she whipped one of them across the room in a frenzied search for her cellphone.

I'm late for school, fuck! You can find every other stupid item in this house but you can't find ONE fucking cellphone!

She shrieked at me. I could hear the tears burbling up her throat.

You see it in my hands all the time!

I didn't bother responding. She would have rendered me useless, even if she didn't really mean it. I wanted to say I was sorry. Really, I did.

I glanced back at the living room seeming more and more undead as the house gave one last, vapid sigh. The furnace whirred in the background, sputtering to heat or cool down a house with no one in it. My stomach joined in and growled ravenously.

Then suddenly, one day, out of the blue, her father turned the lock on me hauled me off to some other house.

So now, here I am. I don't recognize the smells or understand what's happened. I don't know anyone here. I can feel the skin above my snout pulling up and my teeth are showing.

All I can do is wonder: Is it my fault? Where is the mother in all of her suffocating perfume and blonde glory? Where is my brown girl with the laughing curls? She fed me and bathed me and nearly drowned me in all of her heavy, messed up love. Did her love finally dwindle? Where the hell am I? Why wasn't she here to hold me and rub behind my ears?

The last thing she said to me was,

you stupid, clumsy dog. I love you, Drago.

Drago

it was a Sunday morning. probably sometime in May.

i'm in high school, and i hate May.

but that's a totally different story.

anyway…

i awaken,

freshen up,

and head over to my mother's room with some breakfast

to finish watching a movie with her.

the room is empty and about fifteen minutes later,

she saunters in silently,

and shoots me a wary glance.

what's wrong? i ask.

her eyes narrow and she spits. *Why don't you ask your father?*

i bring his coffee and sandwich downstairs.

he freezes when he sees me and blinks,

swivels around in his computer chair.

so i gave your dog away. your mother hated him, so…

his voice trails off.

my mother had just grown warm to his company.

my father always did this—master of manipulation

—always out to make mom look like the bad guy.

i shoved his stupid coffee at him so hard

it spilled over a little onto the computer desk

and plopped the plate in front of him.

i loved that animal with every fiber of my being,

bathed him,

and nurtured him for years.

that dog

was the first consistent figure

i'd had in my life in years,

aside from my mother.

and my father

had just so callously given him away

to some other fucking family

that i didn't even get to meet.

you know,

i'm still not entirely sure what that did to me,

but i still feel it to this day.

he had stolen my best friend.

i still haven't forgiven him.

and part of me still doesn't understand why this affects me so.

Natural Mystic

my father sitting in our basement

listening to old reggae.

he'd puff on a

Cuban cigar and ask me to crack open beers

my father was a tired man

his face once animated was now replaced with

a worn mask from hours of sleeplessness

the creases on his warm face had indicated

that the years had not been so subtle

and unforgivingly desiccated bits of his brown skin

but being able to watch him so

unbothered by anything

—that was a miracle

whatever was eating him

on the inside

would trickle away with the beer

and heavy cigar smoke tickling in his breath

my father with his feet propped up

on his big sofa

looking like papa bear

and reggae was the only music in English that he
truly loved

he had an ear for Bob Marley

and understanding the cadence in his dialect

those evenings were almost ritualistic

he'd kick back wearing an Afrocentric cap
over his melon head
and we would croak and cry out
along with Marley's drawl

like he could almost
fe-ee-eeel Marley's pain

my father
he would *beat time*
on the skin of his congas—
just the way Thomas Roethke's father did

right on his little head

it was the closest I could ever get to my old man:

through music and incense smoke

all tumbling together in the same room

my father teaching me to

listen to each melody

meld into the next

You Were Gone

like my bored ex-boyfriend

like my old German Shepard

gone like the toy I cried over

(can't even remember now which toy it was)

but I searched for that damn thing endlessly,

beneath a heap of dirty laundry, blankets, and *stuff*

I sniffled while rummaging under my bed

hoping,

praying that it was wedged in between

chests and

boxes

and

shoes

and empty cans of soda

and water bottles

but you were gone

gone

like frozen fish

like Pooh's last drop of honey

gone like that stupid necklace I could never find

the one my father gave me when

he left us—for the umpteenth time

you know

the one with the little brown elephant made of
copper

that dangled from its black thread that I'd chew on

half the time it was wet with saliva

and the elephant—discolored and consumed by

rust

you were gone—lost

lost like the hair tie that

vanished from my wrist

when I needed it most

to remove that curtain

of hair from my face

just to get a better look at you

lost like the apartment my family left

behind

you were gone

like supposed best friends from high school

like the cutting grin on my face

like the violin I had

coldly abandoned

left to collect dust, standing wanly

inside of its black, velvet casket

suffocating

and idle

you were gone

like when *Hey Arnold* stopped airing on
Nickelodeon

like when my sticky handfuls of Nilla Wafers
turned to crumbs

like my orange sweater

the one with the zipper that broke

on a Friday the Thirthteenth

after watching a black cat flit across the street

the same one with a deep cappuccino stain

sitting upon my left breast

the one with the cuffs

that smelled like the barks of the trees

just outside my house

you were gone

like seconds

like moments

minutes

hours within

days past

and weeks

months

like sixteen short years spent and wasted

just gone

OH, and P.S. there are so many things I have left to say to you like how beautiful you were and, like, why weren't we together? I'm still in love with a dead guy; *a dead guy.* Why does that sound so wrong? It's not like you were just *some guy.* You were *my* boy. You don't even get it, do you? Ever since they cremated you, Cotard's Syndrome has never felt more real to me.

Do you even know what the fuck that means? It

basically means when you think you're dead, man.

A walking corpse, that's what the fuck that means.

I thought that my heart and my brain were cremated with you. I thought that my flesh was food for maggots at some point. I thought that I was rotting from the inside out because I was convinced that I was some living dead girl thingy. But here's the thing,

I still have you. I have you when we were little. I have you when we were innocent. I will never get to tell you any of these things because right now you and I are stuck in time, sleepily nodding in and out of that stuffy library they'd take us to in second grade, sitting on that Capri Sun-stained carpet, watching the spines of books we won't ever read and inhaling their comforting, stale scent.

Right now, we are still seven years old. We love binge-watching *Cat-Dog,* wolfing down Chips Ahoy cookies with orange juice and cuddling during silent reading.

Right now, you are my favorite part of myself. I have forever here with you the boy who lifted me up and out of the darkest parts of myself.

The end.

The Mute

i'd suffered several instances of sexual abuse before
but one particular night was by far the worst
i was 11 and in my own room
i could have screamed
my folks were right there in the hall
but i was just too scared

you were just a kid, is what my therapist said

i went limp under my perpetrator
and stared off to the side
my eyes finding the first thing
that brought me comfort
and that was my enormous
stuffed rabbit
perched up on the shelf

i stared down at myself from where my bunny was

that night, i saw a little blood

(i thought that i could kill others with my silence.
but i was only killing myself.)

My Cousin Isa

i remember pretending

to understand the lyrics

from her favorite band

because i so badly needed to look cool in her eyes

sugarcult was the name—

they sounded like

they were the type of white boys

to talk in circles

and cry about beaten-up girlfriends

their voices oozed through the pores

of her stereo and inflated

those angsty teen walls

until it suffocated us both

until eventually it grew on me

"pretty girl is suffering while he confesses
everything, pretty soon she'll figure out what his
intentions were about"

i remember watching artless porn with her

and stiff, plastic body parts slapping around

big dicks on a 90's Dell computer,

the monitor as big as my head at the time

the mouse had a sticky scroller and the keys were in
a disarray of offset grays

and i remember reading through smutty Buffy fan
fiction

for the first time

Isa read:

*"and Angel shoved his throbbing cock into Buffy,
screaming 'i am not a eunuch!'"*

i pressed my thighs together and licked my lips,
eyes glued to the screen

i wanted more

the warmth that pooled in my stomach and melted
between my thighs—

after shuffling upstairs, our panties tight and moist,

we wondered what to do with ourselves next

she watched *Days of our Lives*, spreading herself on
her parents' bed like a starfish

suddenly, i pulled my arms far back and punched
the pillows

i crawled onto the bed with a slimy little grin

and commenced to hop up and down like an ape,

wrinkling the sheets with my feet

all the while, i made sure my eyes never left hers—

my tousled curls bouncing and laughing with me

in between leaps, i made these animalistic grunts
and groans

that rippled from my throat

she stopped me short, wide eyed, and

demanded that i stop

i still never lost eye contact and watched her,
panting

pleased

finally, i asked her with a soft smile

if she ever recognized those sounds

coming from this room

late at night

what do you even know about any of that? she
shook her head in disbelief, laughing

This Is How I Died

i am eleven years old—

a gold cross caught between clenched teeth
bending over an empty box of Capri Sun pouches
toes curling on cool tiles on my kitchen floor
peering out of a barely open window

the balmy breeze breathing in through the black
screen,
pulling on my shaky fingers gripping the wooden
sill
as i shut my eyes, bit down hard, and begged for
God to feel it, too

my elbows trembled like gaunt legs under a
nightstand ready to give out

i can't remember how many fingers were inside of
me
but it felt like i was being split in half down the
middle—

fucked with dry rubber gloves

every time the bitch pushed and pulled out again,
i could feel myself dissolving

i prayed that she would fuck me so hard with her
fingers
that i would just disappear

never mind my inner thighs, later that night—
wet, bright and very much alive, slick with blood

i was dead—don't care what anyone else says

my ghost walked through chalk-white walls
until i burned holes in the floors

my spirit, which took my once physical form like
haunted memory foam,
wandered aimlessly in an ever-perplexed,
endless loop

sauntering in this strange in-between-ness that is
and isn't my house

thirteen years later,
now words don't make sense anymore when people
talk to me

garbled, slurred—half the time i don't catch most of
what someone is trying to tell me
their faces start to look like puzzle pieces
especially where their mouths are

their voices fade

but whether i was eleven or twenty-four,
the sun was still shining

it's always, already, and still shining—forever

and my ghostly frame will never feel the gentle sun

on my shoulders ever again
i am always eleven

always staring out of that kitchen window
watching when the dark, starry blanket
starts to spill like ink over dreams of orange and
pink in the sky

as i twist and writhe in spirit, i watch the seasons
grow, bloom, die, emerge again—
the trees shedding their dry leaves as the year
slowly comes apart before me

a deadened winter

eager spring

angry summer

still eleven, her fingers curved inside of me
like she's trying to pluck the scared cries out of my
cunt

it's like she doesn't even realize she's fingering a
dead girl

i so badly wished for death to come and take me
soft and easy
so it did

and this is how i died

If A Body Catch A Body

Sweet milk, baby breath whispers,
squirms beside me restlessly, and leans in
"I can't sleep," he blinks.

I don't shudder away from him—not anymore.
Instead, I shimmy under his fleece blanket,
and swim back up to the surface.

I emerge—up and out of my cocoon,
gracefully
and wrap my arms around his tiny frame—
after having morphed myself into a mother,
a sibling,
a cousin,
a nurturer.

He presses his tiny, sweaty palms against
my cheeks—magical beings: children.
I smile now, willing to grow intimate
with the wide-eyed child before me.
My chest swells, overwhelmed and
suddenly dizzy with his bouncing innocence.

More, he demands.
Again, he squeals, and erupts into peals of
laughter. He is consumed with giggles, and I try,
as delicately as I can, to absorb it all.
Another one, he cries.
Together, he sings at me.

All the while, I give in,
pushing back a mountain of curls
away from his forehead:
Here's your popsicle, I say.
It's late, I declare.
Fine, Ty, fine—but only ONE more, I sigh.

At bedtime, we both cry
when I slap together
the covers of Peter Pan and tuck it away.
Ty shrieks, hot tears springing from his eyes.
He demands seconds.

It's too soon, I sob,
knowing well that
my time was robbed once.
I don't have enough time—
I didn't have enough time
with the babies.

Time had gobbled up
what little vestiges of innocence
I had floating around inside of me.

So I sprint after the children,
coming through the rye—carefully,
desperately tossing my arms out
to catch them before they topple over
out of their cradle.

Ty closes his eyes,
eyebrows furrowed together
and sniffling.

I weep silently to myself
because every grown
already knows why
Peter never, ever wanted
to grow up.

Sweet Dreams

I was born to wear flip-flops
and feel the thick plastic chafing
the skin between my big toe and
my middle toe—
born to show off my freshly done pedicure
and bat my mascara-caked lashes upward
to flirt with the sun.

And I already talked about how
I was born to never catch a robin,
in all of its velvety, crimson coat and fleeting
glory—
an unobtainable, fiery little angel.
And even though I spent hours
on a summer's afternoon
fixing bird traps with my father
trying to take what wasn't even mine,
I always knew deep down it would never be.

Some days we contemplated

on grabbing our BB rifle and

would wait at the window, watching eagerly.

Then we backed out the very last minute

when we saw that tiny, vermillion creature

bathing itself in the pink evening sunlight,

fluttering its wings nervously as water from the
fountain

sprung from its feathers like slivers of ice.

I was born to kiss boys on balmy summer nights

with a little bravery from Bacardi on my breath

and then regret it in the mornings.

I was born to tell a story

with the tip of a cigarette burning between my
lips—

all glassy-eyed and singing off-key

and wondering where the hell my life is headed.

I was born to drink in the nightlife
with salt and lemon on the side.

I was born to join the party
and make everyone there raise a toast
to whatever it is they're all anxious about
and everyone will cheer—
hoping for something good to beam down
on their lives
no matter the situation they're in.
And all of them will believe in something
with all of that liquor swimming in their system,
dripping from their throbbing pores
and happily filling in their hearts and stomachs—
their livers crying out for help all the while.

Hitting Puberty

She's old enough to bleed now
So she's old enough to breed
Old enough to show just how
A man relieves his needs

She's old enough to bleed
Old enough to realize this:
Old enough to stick this tampon
Through her second pair of lips

She's old enough to peek
And know what's hiding behind doors
She's old enough to know if
Daddy left them for a whore

She's old enough to drink
And she's old enough to fight
Old enough for kissing
And she's old enough to try

She's old enough to plead
And she's old enough to beg
She's old enough to let a man
Feel up between her legs

She's old enough to bleed
She's old enough to breed
She's old enough to raise her chin
And scrap her dirty knees

Old enough to flaunt
And I'm old enough to tease
I'm old enough to beat upon
Your nasty fucking meat

I'm old enough to bleed
I'm old enough to breed
I'm old enough to swallow
And I'm old enough to scream

Old enough to snap
Old enough to run
Old enough for acting up
And talking back to some
I'm old enough to freak
Old enough for fun
I'm old enough to love and leave
A man after he comes

I'm old enough to bleed
I'm old enough to breed
I'm old enough to tear out hearts
And stomp them as I please

Muted Disgust

I tried to explain it to them before:

"Both of my parents are Puerto Rican; however, my father is what one would consider a black Latino and my mother a white Latina. So, out on the street, they just look like a typical interracial Black-White couple—while I always tagged along, labeled as their little mulatto child (which is a pretty sick term if you ask me)."

White kids blinked at me blankly. Black kids just frowned.

I guess one group thought I was trying to fit in by accentuating my whiteness. The other thought I was trying to erase my blackness.

Too black, too white? I never really knew.

There was always this discomfort in my family's eyes from my father's side—like they could hardly bear to look my mother and me in the face. Yet, sometimes they studied us (me and my mother's side of the family) like a menagerie of pompous White people. But we were far from that. Nevertheless, my Black side was utterly disgusted with me. I could tell by the pinched look around their eyes when they forced smiles at me that they couldn't stand having me around. The fact that I was half White had, ultimately, convinced them to remain cold with me.

I noticed the racial tension, especially, the day my grandmother from my Black side grabbed me by the arm and gave me a couple of good blows across my back, then shook me angrily.

You think you're better? *She hissed.*

She said this more as a statement rather than a question. Then she'd ask me, what's your problem?

As though it were my fault—as if I knew the answer to her inane questions.

They would grimace at family gatherings at my mother and made her feel excluded from all jokes, games, and meals. They were like a clique. And ashamed at the same time.

So my mother and I remained these incongruous freckles, peppered across their blackness. We were a disturbance to them, a flaw. And I was living proof of their miscegenation. My caramel-colored skin and "good hair" spat right in their eyes. To them, my presence was mocking and unwanted—at least that's how they made me feel, and they did a wonderful job at it.

Whatever happened to blood is thicker than water? I guess in this case skin is tougher than love, and since I don't look like them, I'm not allowed in. I'm not tough like them. I'm not one of them. Through their eyes, I will always be the marginalized half-breed, the strange mulatto.

A mistake.

The Nightgown

i put on my mother's nightgown the other
morning—
i'm not sure why
i just did

i found it draped over the armrest of the sofa in the
living room
delicate as a wilted petal

so i picked it up carefully
and decided to slip it on

i felt like i was wearing her skin
and almost instantly my bones began to ache

i felt a sudden urge to scrapbook and crochet
and i could feel myself floating throughout the
house
solving everyone's problems

and her essence sank in my stomach
so heavily

my shoulders started to feel like rained-on grocery
bags

so i peeled it off of myself and shuddered,
dropping it back onto the sofa

maybe i might have actually dreamt all of that

yeah, it probably was a dream...

II

The Shorts

—Because less is more, I guess

Sometimes she wakes up on a perfectly beautiful day and thinks to herself as she squints at the sun,

Today is a good day to die.

He had this gift of being able to look at me not from the outside in, but starting from the inside and then out—right through me. Not an ounce of judgment in his eyes.

I am a sad spook—the ghost child destined to leave one poisoned void only to haunt another.

Well, I don't believe that, her partner swears.

I will grow and seep inside of you like how roots sew themselves into the soil. And then you will start to rot. I do this to everything I touch, *the ghost child threatened.*

Fine, if you say so.

I like picturing couples fuck. Not because I get off
on it or anything. I mean, sometimes I do.
Depending on the couple, you know? But that's
beside the point. I enjoy picturing them because I
just like to wonder what they look like when they're
completely vulnerable. What happens to their hair,
their breathing, and their skin when they're all
flustered and wanting and wet? Who are they when
they're stripped of any and all inhibition? Where do
they go when they cum?

Sax

Eggplant, violet, gray:

Hands heavy on my back as they fell
roses, blood

and my chest caving in.

I had a dress on the calendar
for a springy Tuesday.

It was perfect.

But when Tuesday came,
when the sun spilled across the walls of my room

blazing through each sliver of the blinds,

the timing was all the way wrong.

My liver was gone
and I was disillusioned.

Her hands wash over me in the morning—wisdom
pours out of them like fresh sunlight for the soul
(this is my mother).

She complained to me
in a low voice,
       blinking slow,
       twirling pale liquid gold Sauterne
in her glass,

about how her geometric shag rugs
used to be oh-so-expensive once.

She sat sideways on her knees,
one side of her hip
       rolling out
from her waist like the
       grooves
       of sand dunes
       as she drew out her words
—tongue too thick with wine.

This half-feline, half-woman
sports a tangerine scarf with
70s eurynome floral patterns,

a black cardigan with thumb holes,

and gray and black moth marled slacks.

The dim light

filtered through

the blue pleated cloth lampshade

     and hit her face

     in a soft, suffocating way,

just like the sun briefly caught

     in her almond eyes

     through a tear in the blinds.

And coincidentally,

     that too-stuffy,

     cool blue light

unveiled a palm-sized bruise

that glinted painfully bright,

right upon

     the apple of her cheek.

It was damp,

caked with a foundation

that was barely

    a few

        shades

            lighter

than her true skin tone.

I squinted,

searched her face

for the answers I wanted,

    inhaled sharply,

ready her to ask her

that exhausting question:

    "How?"—

Finally,

before I could gather

the energy to do so,

    she explained to me,

        "It was the door, darling.

        The,

uh,

sliding glass door."

Only one corner of her mouth
pulled up
into a half-hearted smile,
combing through strands
of flyaway hairs
with fumbling fingers.

And then there it was:

her
eyes
dropped.

It was
almost
convincing

the way she

wafted her hand

upward,

motioning to the bruise

      in this disgustingly cavalier manner.

But the tremor in her voice,

the hazy, and glossed-over gaze

in her eyes,

the unmistakable uncertainty

in her not-so-sober state of stammering

gave it

all

away.

Every time I try to picture you, I shatter a thousand times. Because I feel like your face is slowly dissolving with time. And to no longer feel the pain of losing you is to forget you entirely.

The wind is catching us! she shrieked, running with the leaves whirling around her messy ponytail. She tripped over wood chips, landing palms first and laughed (this is a pre-k student).

I'm in love with dead men, apparently.

I have them mounted all over my walls.

The Beatles—well, they're basically halfway dead.

Let's see… I've got Jimi Hendrix.

Michael Jackson.

Elvis Presley.

Charlie Chaplin.

The Three Stooges.

James Dean.

And I feel funny most of the time, having to step out of the shower in nothing but a towel and they're just there. Staring down at me lifelessly. That's what I get for falling in love with dead guys.

Sometimes, while I do have good memories of my father, there are others I can't quite recall—almost like they're more of a bad, sick feeling rather than an actual memory. That worries me. But just when I feel like most of my good memories with him are fading, one of them will hit me and I start smiling again.

Like when he told me about the time when he was a toddler and he enjoyed destroying his pacifiers.

Or when he looked at a rain puddle for the first time, he thought that he was going to fall through them forever.

It was refreshing to hear him remember things like that—made him seem more human and less of an asshole.

Like, damn, he was actually small and vulnerable once.

Adulting is...

being placed on hold for the majority of the phone calls you make.

Adulting is…

having your toe itch while driving and attempting to scratch it while trying not to crash.

Adulting is…

wondering when your bad luck will run out.

Adulting is…

getting excited/surprised about something new whenever you go back to the dollar store.

Adulting is…

finding cool ways to fold your bath/face towels and ecstatically texting your friends about this new discovery.

Adulting is…

wanting to go out but also passing out by 9:38 p.m.

Be the goofy smile on my face.

Be the smile on my face that makes me dizzy.

Be the smile on my face that makes people wonder what I've been up to.

Listening to a joke

Feeding a child while crying

Having a cup of coffee while breaking up with someone

Fucking someone in pitch black darkness

Plucking out flowers from between your legs

Swallowing a butterfly

Crying mascara-stained tears over onions

The feathers from her scarf carved me from the inside out, and her shadows slipped in and out of me.

Her fingers are dexterous and search for invisible answers she thinks are engraved under my sizzling skin. I wonder what it says. She hasn't told me her theories yet.

The other night her fingers disappeared and melted inside of me. They twisted and pulled and all I could do was writhe around, moan helplessly beneath her crushing weight. My breathlessness felt so incredibly freeing.

Sometimes all she has to do is lace her fingers into mine and suddenly I have sex hair for no reason. Uncontrollable. Inevitable. Wild.

And then her lips...

holyshiticantbreatheicantthink

I know that I'm with him. But, girl, you're the first thing that I think about when I wake up in the morning—**not him**. You're the one holding my heart, ready to crush it under your boot heel.

And I know that most girls wanted to BE her or be her best friend.

I just remember *wanting to be hers*.

You are my favorite kind of love. Is that so wrong?

In my version of hell, all of the strippers have nightmares while they dance.

I hate removing my contacts.

It enhances every other unspoken fear I have

into an even blurrier viewfinder.

I'd never considered myself a rebel, but I sure have enjoyed fantasizing being the accomplice of one…

Your breath can read my mind, tongue can taste my fear, ears wait in the sky. And you sleep with one eye. Then you tie your sins like laces and lightly wrap them around my ankles.

She said she fell in love with the way I write, said she wanted to marry someone

who writes like Margorie does. She was blushing when she said that last thing.

Her ivory skin on fire in the evening summer sun. I can't forget that.

My heart pulsated in my throat, unable to keep my eyes off of her lips so close to mine.

Red like a crimson ribbon.

All the while, she gazed up at me with sex eyes.

One of these things doesn't belong...

It's strange to find a pair of spotted panties or a muddy shower cap in the middle of the sidewalk in a rural, quiet town. But it's not so uncommon to see those items lying somewhere on a college campus.

Just like it's really not the weirdest thing to see shoefiti coughed up everywhere in the city, but it is a little out of the ordinary to see it in the suburbs.

She lingers in my blankets—

tangled like a shoelace.

She wants everything.

So I say, *fine.*

Fine, here. Have the world.

If there is a hell, I know that I deserve to burn in it for a while. Some people will really study me when I say that and say, "Come on, you aren't that shitty of a person. There are others who have done way worse."

And I'm like, so what? That doesn't absolve me of my sins or lessen the severity of what I've done. Sure, if you had to pick between which is worse—stealing someone's television set or killing someone—you'd probably pick the petty crime because taking a life is just savagery, right?

Nectar

Imagine. And then I want to remember. I feel like chilly, blue rooms, Chinese food in the dark with you, comfortable couches and all of Rudy's belongings right where they should be. I feel like a few hours of Sailor Moon, and the blinds half-open, or maybe half-closed. My pen asks me politely, later in the afternoon to bleed. My fingernails are but too rough to scrape against the sky this day— much too dreary for something like that. When the sun is out, perhaps, then I'll take advantage of the horrifying—

These sleepless, erotic little cherubs smile at me in my dreams. And what was the point of it all? I have only 26% battery left on my phone, and still 3 and half hours of work ahead of me. A Twix and some ocean spray, strawberry kiwi cocktail juices keep me going. My Band-Aids with orange and white labels from a doctor glisten in my purse like candy corn. Don't cry.

Just think about sable-haired Snow White and the way she cuts gracefully into the laps of the old blue, sweet, turned-in toes gliding clumsily over the plastic seams. I have never seen her up close before. Beautiful. And where is Laura today?

Nectar

Noise

sometimes
i wish i could bash my skull
into a notebook

and watch all of the noise spill out onto the pages
like paint

that would be easier than having to actually pen it
all
and live it all over again

Rape

i wonder how i could describe what getting raped is
like—

like a tree getting skinned of its bark
or a dog getting its butt beaten bloody
or house plants being flipped the fuck over in a
home invasion
—wet dirt still stuck to the grooves of thick boot
heels
or having to hold your own guts in your hands and
staring down at them

how could i possibly describe something like that?

III

Spells

Not Really

*I don't believe for a second that you're truly
beautiful, but I'm drawn to you like a moth to the
flame. It isn't until I have you down on paper that
you become someone that maybe I'd like to get to
know. I admire you from afar even though you make
me physically sick. My stomach rolls in on itself
with the thought of us holding hands or even our
arm hairs grazing against mine, but I have to hold
back from sitting down beside you. You're a force of
nature and it's like when you move, the world
moves with you—the sun moves with you, the sky
moves with you, fruit juice and flies move with you,
eyes move with you, girls and guys move with you.*

But I am never really moving with you.

*As a matter of fact, I'm trying desperately to swim
against the current, but when everything is moving
against me and you're the only source of energy
and light they're supposed to feed on, that's when
things become a little dicey. So every time you open
your mouth, I feel like I'm drowning in a mudslide.
It's not that I don't mind having my insides caked
with your muck, because I still enjoy it.*

*But you pop a nerve in me when you flutter in, in
that stupid way on your broken wing.*

I want to make you beautiful, and I really do try

*when I write about you. I make myself believe that
we belong to each other. And then I mold you into
something you aren't, but I can still make others
believe that the very air I breathe is all yours first—
that I hold my breath and wait for you to inhale first
before I can even think about breathing again.*

*Truth is, you're the envious whisper at every party
that spreads like lice and slips into everyone's
drink. You're the angry, anxious slurs of sloppy,
drunken girls and pissed off, horny boys looking for
love by snatching fistfuls of panties.*

*You're the ugly, sharp turn at a curb and the ear-
splitting screech that comes after. And you let the
crumbs from your bullshit fall inside of me.*

*You're the evil, insecure snicker in a quiet room.
You're the bully and the bullied.*

I want to make you beautiful.

*I want to fold you, crush you, and sprinkle what's
left of you inside of a cocoon. And when all is said
and done, I want you to come out as this painfully
beautiful butterfly.*

*And when you do, I want to cup you in my hands.
Then stick a few needles in you and pin you to a
canvas. Finally, I'll tell people, "It came to me,
died, then I glossed it up and here it is. Isn't it*

beautiful?"

Guess what? Even though I feel as though I don't deserve to make something beautiful in this world, I put my hands on you anyway. And may God damn me if I don't make it my mission in life, until the day my heartstrings snap, to make you fucking beautiful.

Through the Backyards

I ordered pizza while I clipped my fingernails. My thoughts sailed, out of time and reason, hiding in special corners of you. I leaned back into the sofa, flat-footed, seated, drinking a soda. Through the windows beamed the warm sun, was there pink in the sky? Certainly looked it. I purposely hit call to hear your voice but all I got were the eerie chords of a missed conversation. Then out of the blue, I could have sworn I heard you. But it was just your stupid voicemail. Of course you weren't there, the worst situation I've ever been placed in, I can't face it. My train of thought derails, jolts, reeks, and my knees are frail. Where are my keys, fuck it, I've failed again, peanut, tell me all your secrets and then please don't feel bad if I can't, won't, don't find the right words to say right away. Please, forgive me.

Car Ride

My thumb is dry. I run it across the blanket slowly. And it sounds like summer.

It reminds me of the wind in my hair, the sun in my eyes, and cotton candy stuck to my fingers.

I was so scared to swallow the pink wisps—thinking that they were patches of clown hair. I thought I might choke.

But my cousin's hand—her fingers trickled over my thigh like the fluttering sun on our car ride from the carnival.

And she breathed, let it melt in your mouth… first it's sweet and then it's gone, *she promised me.*

Okay, *I trusted. And moments later, its cottony, sugary sweetness dissolved on my tongue and vanished inside of me.*

I gasped, magic.

The Salsa Song

His life is like a sad salsa song, his voice like velvet and full of forgotten melodies. So I took it upon myself to one day share the stories that the bruises on his heart can't tell.

Like Daisy

she told me something beautiful
in a hideous way
and i was confused

whether she was
serious or not;
her lips seemed playful

but her twisted smile
said otherwise
as her eyes glistened

with a glint of anger
in them, they flashed
like knives

the reflection in
them danced like a
cacophony of dazzling sequins

and her breath still
strong and sweet with
Tanqueray before 8pm

…giggling and merciless

turned on like
fire
just a thin sheen over her skin

as she perspired delicately

then met my
jeans and touched
my arm, wetting her lips

she leaned in over me
heart thrumming in my ears
hissing something like

how do i taste?

Royal Skeleton

catch me when I fall
like a snowflake on your tongue
and you relish in the cold
while my crystals fizzle gold

color me in blue
as i melt inside of you
give me winter—bitter wind
in your oily dreams, i blend

you already knew me—
we're a billion
we're forever

you whistle right through me
we're a billion
we're forever

split me open to
find the crevices in you
that you do not know are there
mark the spots you think are bare

shatter on my sleeve
be the budding, balmy breeze
dress me up in red
watch me twirling in your head

you already knew me—

we're a billion
we're forever

you whistle right through me
we're a billion
we're forever

The Blizzard

My mother says my mind is a blizzard. She also compared my emotions to a volcano and my heart to a tornado.

She says my room is a hurricane and that my closet is so messy, I just might have a few cadavers lying around in there.

Anyway—the storms?

I noticed they're all massive calamities—these uncontrollable, unpredictable forces of nature.

They're destructive and haunting—almost beautiful. All of that graceful bullshit.

And I liked that idea: being dangerous and beautiful. But I don't know if that's exactly what she meant.

I don't think it was.

The Black Sheep

This generation of the devout Chain family had four boys birthed by Wendy Chain, the daughter of a marine, taxi driver, landlord, engineer, law school student, and forester. Wendy and her husband decided that, one day, these four Chain church boys would marinade in the Lord's grace and spread His heavenly word.

And so, the Chain boys grew, softened by Wendy's grace, their bottoms tendered with a wooden spoon, and shaken with the vehement roar that erupted from their father's Mormon lungs.

There's Abel, Eli, Jeremiah, and Gabriel—each of the boys taller, stronger, and handsomer than the next. They're boys with split irises, russet brown and blonde tufts of hair, and bodies built like sinewy lumberjacks.

But the eldest, Gabriel, in all of his 6'3 glory, stands alone. And I was swept up off of my feet. I can imagine Wendy wailing in the labor room while this 8-pound baby boy tore her apart.

Out of the four Chain church boys, I had the pleasure of falling for the black sheep—the one who ironically said (and I'm just going to paraphrase this), to hell with religion.

I can understand why he thinks that way. However, I cannot and do not wish to imagine his terror, being surrounded by four stained-glass walls of a church that chided him with those horrible, sobbing figures, those grey-scaled gargoyles glowering down at him, and parents who scolded him, subtly imposing these God-fearing ideas. They encouraged him to wash it all down with a flock of hypocrites who can't seem to wait before making it down the church steps to gossip about so and so's skirt being two-inches too short or Pastor Dan's affair with the Wendell family's eldest daughter. I'd get pretty sick of that shit, too.

While Gabriel's younger brother Jeremiah currently spends his time in Brazil doing precisely what Wendy and her husband had predicted before his birth, which is spreading the Word of the Lord to those who apparently haven't been saved yet (though, I'm not sure what they're being saved from exactly, and I would like to discover the purpose of this spiritual endeavor someday), Gabriel dedicates his time to locksmithing and showing sweaty, stinking, curious boys the art of archery, hunting, and probably the slicing, dicing and shooting of other things in the Wisconsin woods he knows so well.

Every year, those smelly little boy scouts warmly welcome him, practically wagging their tails. From what I hear, they see stars for Gabriel. There was even one little, redheaded hellion who refused to cooperate during their archery class, so Gabriel calmly chucked the boy's arrows deep into the woods for the boy to run his rude ass out and retrieve them. Gabriel did this for some time and if not by, I guess, God's will, then I don't know what. One sacred day, the boy succumbed and bowed his head to Gabriel with respect.

I gave Gabriel a nickname—my lumberjack. And it truly was fitting because he had one folded, weather-beaten, leather hat and this weird, green-ish, khaki-colored jacket. Hell, he even got the beard, and let me tell you, it was glorious. I'm talking Jeffrey Dean Morgan full on beard.

Anyway, he was wearing that baby shit-colored jacket the night we met. I remember very gently patting his arm and inhaling the musk from his 15-hour shift, the faint, lingering scent of firewood, and something like a coppice-spice cologne. Heavenly.

He understood the whisper of warm Wisconsin wood as his gigantic, weathered palms ran deftly over tree rings and pine-scented plywood boards—fumbled, as though decoding something written in braille or ancient hieroglyphs.

While we stood side by side, he breathed life into an angry bonfire with a little liquor on his breath—his blue and green split irises painting those flirtatious flecks of fire. His heart lies deep in the Wisconsin undergrowth, among the sugar pines, inside of a grill, and overlooking the twin lakes. Mine is probably somewhere inside of the Metra fleeting through Chicago, marveling at the immensity of the skyscrapers, enthralled by the skyline's thousands of brilliant, winking lights stretched out across Lake Michigan. I like to wear the city confidently like the little bold, black dress every woman keeps tucked away in her closet behind her work attire and casual weekend wear. Gabriel buried himself out in the country.

His hands. I couldn't hold onto them enough. While those rough, rugged hands choked up on an ax to chop down wood, I would write on those trees. We're both tree lovers, he said. And I never thought of us that way before, but it's true. He grazed the wood down into tabletops, knives, and splinters for a bonfire. His hands twisted and tore through thorns, but they could be gentle as ever. His thumbs made little circles on my palms and cradled me like minding the head of an infant. He had these perfect, silky blonde hairs peppered across the top of his tanned hands. They became caked with grime, paint, and dirt. But they never stopped being sensitive, and I just couldn't lace my fingers between his enough.

Meanwhile, around the bonfire, my blood burned white hot, scintillating under my skin and burrowing deep into his brown brow. In that broken light, he was almost beautiful, careful with his words but eager and growing braver by the second, thanks to a little Bacardi.

My first time was in a tent. I had a lot of ideas and expectations about losing my virginity—nothing too far-fetched, but I did have a few requirements, if you will, in mind. I didn't picture rose petals scattered across the floor or a dimly lit room with Marvin Gaye's crooning in the background and wine that would cost me my entire summer stipend.

Ideally, I saw myself losing it someplace quiet and not too spacious with someone special enough— maybe a little Bob Marley drawling to his sensual Stir It Up.

But we don't live in an ideal world.

So instead, I found myself at a campsite in Wisconsin just before the on-season activity. That was where I tumbled around inside of a too-small tent with a 6 foot 3 man that resembled a very hot lumberjack. Rather than Chardonnay, we indulged in a bottle of Crown Royal.

We had no music to accompany our quickened breaths and dampened skin—nothing but the active chirping of crickets. Nothing but the droplets of spittlebugs onto the mesh and plastic cover of the tent. Absolutely nothing but our bodies, nature, and

*a hardened surface with thick blankets wrapped
around us in the early afternoon.*

Now you have something special to tell your friends
later, *he smirked. I tilted my head at him as we
climbed out of the tent.*

What are you talking about? *I inquired softly.*

Bet none of them have ever lost it in a tent before.
*And he winked. I couldn't believe he said that, and
almost instantly I was consumed with laughter.*

*We still had the taste of sleep in our mouths and
tousled bed heads, but we were both restless. And I
had an itch. He rolled over and gently squeezed my
arms. His hands were tender and slow like kneading
dough.*

*The spittlebugs continued to spill themselves all
over our tent. They formed a white, fresh froth on
the braches that sprouted out needle leaves. Every
so often, I felt a cool welcome trickle onto my
forehead, dissolve into my curls, or slither down
onto my forearm.*

*Some days Gabriel would dive unashamedly into a
story about chopping wood, cracking locks, or
shaving down keys for people, and I'd just blink at
him and nod. But I smiled because he got it. He
knew the ins and outs of all sorts of knobs and*

locks, and I think it was easier for him that way.
Keys and locks were way more predictable than I
probably would have ever been. They even come
with a manual—not like me, unfortunately. I don't
come with one of those.

He wouldn't have been able to pick me apart like a
lock. He couldn't flip through a pamphlet that says,
"If you twist Marge's side just a quarter of an inch
and then probe her once in the back, she'll give in."
There is no YouTube video with instructions on how
to pop open my hood and fix me. I have dents and
scratches, my muffler is fucked, my engine won't
run right, and my tires and rims have gone to hell.

Sometimes, girls want someone to be a repairman
for them and clean everything out that's inside, fix it
up and make it pretty. Maybe they think that way
because of those stupid Hallmark cards that usually
read something along the lines of, "You are the key
to my heart." Like, here's a key to my heart, do
what you will with it.
But I didn't want Gabriel to act like a key to my
anything. I didn't need him to feel pretty with
myself. Quite the contrary, I wanted him to find a
way—to create the perfect lock with those bulky
hands, to seal all of those dark and slimy, cob-
webbed spaces in me only after he'd seen them.

What I wanted was his scratchy beard at the nape of
my neck. I wanted to cut wood, learn to shoot with a

rifle, and spot all of the constellations he knew. I wanted to listen to the laps of the riverbed with him and the sizzling of a grill.

I wanted to stand beside him before a bonfire, half enveloped in the shadows and be singing over Pink Floyd and his hoarse voice until my lungs were sore. I wanted to know what it was like with him in the woods, to scavenge through old, Native American grounds, find the haunted Wendigo rock, groan with the sway of his hammock, sweat inside of a tent, hum with the cicadas while our sighs dripped with fresh spit from the bugs tucked in between those frothy bristles of a sugar pine nearby.

I wanted the summer forever with him, and I wanted all of these things, all at once until I forgot about the slimy, dark spaces he closed up—until I learned to tame those hungry demons that dwell in there.

But I realized that I couldn't put that burden on him. Not on that terrified, racist church boy. No. I only had one summer with him, and that was all we needed. It was the best.

Snake, Honey, and Thaw

Out in the woods today, early in the crisp, silent morning, he found a snake slithering surreptitiously in the shrubs just behind our tent—ready to throw us off of our trail. It was caked entirely in mud, but he stopped short, his eyes narrowing onto the wiry thing. He seized the animal in one swift motion and trapped it with the end of his stick. The splinters on the edge of the branch jutted out like hair lightly brushed by static.

The thing thrashed violently for less than a second and ceased almost immediately. Now it's muscles curled slowly through memory and reaction. With enormous, rough, rugged hands he tore the skin from its thin, muscular form, peeling away—the juices dripped from its insides like thawing meat or honey and sounded like the glue of a Band-Aid ripping from skin.

Bullies

I was in preschool, and there was this little boy in my class named Matthew. Matthew had a learning disability; even I knew this as a child. He was our age, but didn't quite talk like us and he moved a little slower than everyone else. He was one of those children where you could tell right off the bat that something just wasn't quite right. However, one of the young teachers there at the school was irritated by Matthew's odd behavior. Rather than setting him aside to take care of him or contacting his parents, she sat Matthew upon a stool in front of the entire preschool class, pointed to Matthew and said,

Everyone point at Matthew and laugh. And if I see anyone who isn't laughing at him, then you're going to join him up there and we'll all laugh at you, too.

The Jellies

My mother always has pet names for me. She uses them interchangeably. When she's feeling playful, I'm her skinny bones. When she's being witty, I'm the Pink Panther. Before bed, I'm always her pussycat. But there is one that seems to stick for whatever reason.

Jellyfish.

Of all the long-limbed pet names, she particularly enjoys calling me this one. She says my arms and legs are lumbering and languid like one.

And so, it was several years ago on my 20th birthday that she surprised me with a trip to the Shedd Aquarium. She handed me a pamphlet that read "Special Exhibit: The Jellies."

A lot of them were about the size of my pinky nail— perfect, tiny, transparent bodies sifting seamlessly inside of their tanks. I braced myself as they slithered in, interrupting the frantic, synchronized little dance of other small fish around them.

Blue, fleshy veins sprawled across their pulpous, umbrella-like scalps—they pumped and floated gracefully, cutting through the salted water.

I refused to let this one drift by, so I pulled out my attachable micro-lens for my phone and got it close enough to the tank, then finally snapped the photo shakily before it vanished among the others again.

Its deft little limbs were lost again with all of the other stringy bodies. Finally, it was out of my sight, swallowed by the enormity of the tank. The flecks of brown, pink, and orange flickered still over its slimy body.

What a small yet terrifying and impressive animal, I thought. I wanted to be like them—flowing listlessly like a sinewy storm—pleasing to the eye, but vicious to the touch.

Like When

the bulb breaks
and the house shakes
and the storm rolls in
and the walls cave in

like when the water boils
and the cold wires coil
and the hot rice—it pops
and the relic clock stops

like the beach, when the scorching sand sizzles—
a 4th of July sparkler fizzles
and the violent waves—they collide
and the summer winds give a sigh

like when the languid leaves tremble—
a ball of nerves disassemble
and barren branches sway
and aged roots give way

like when palms slap,
and knuckles crack
when an itch is scratched
and two fingers snap

like when a stomach churns
and the one candle burns
and the smoke dies slow
and the tides ride low

like when wet petals shrivel
the classic spin top swivels
and the rigorous rains let up—
the water spills over that cup

like when the spoiled wood splits
and then the weakened dam bursts
and like the firefly's dwindling glow…

is how hard she cums and how soft she goes.

Claire's Sort-Of Sonnet

Her head is low as I watch her face,
I sit across from her and think,
As she clumsily spills her drink
Quiet, and studiously in her place,
Her eyes are depthless, glossy and soft
She staggers gracefully and comes near
Puts her hand on my chest, and her lips to my ear
Yearning and searching for something she's lost

A lover or someone she can put to rest
She sways and sashays unsteadily
Attempting to dance in her summer dress
Not in her right mind, she slips away stealthily

Consequently, I must confess
That later I'll wake up from this dream

Birdie's Verse

Dimpled back with milky breath
In the morning, nothing left

No more tears to mask the shame
From the murky blue we came

Scrape the dust, rise from the ash
From the undergrowth we dashed

Picture me in something fun—
Wearing nothing but the sun

Box the fear and close the gate
Crack the sky and cry my name

Where did you come from?
Unlike you, I know where the sun sets

How do you live, love?
Out of the blue, all drenched in mud steps

I was born to never catch a robin
I was born to kiss the boys—leave them forgotten

I was born to burn the ants
I was born to leap from the jungle gym and dance

Can we share our skin?
Can we shed and wear each other's past?

Can we shed our skin?
Can we shed our skin like snakes and wear each
other's past?
Just for a while.

Should we pick ourselves apart?
And try to glue ourselves back together?

Are we one or are we nothing at all?